This book belongs to:

_____

PASSAGES
for
CONSOLATION

INSPIRATIONAL KEEPSAKES
FROM LONGMEADOW PRESS:

Proverbs for Today

Psalms for Today

Reflections from Jesus

Passages for Consolation

PASSAGES
for
CONSOLATION

Edited by Michael Myers

LONGMEADOW PRESS

Published by Longmeadow Press, 201 High Ridge Road, Stamford, CT 06904. All rights reserved. No part of this book may be reproduced or utilized in any form or by any means, electronic or mechanical, including photocopying, recording or by any information storage and retrieval system, without permission in writing from the Publisher.

Jacket design by Lisa Amoroso
Interior design by Lisa Amoroso
ISBN: 0-681-41891-5
Printed in U.S.A.
First Edition
0 9 8 7 6 5 4 3 2 1

Love

In the LANGUAGES of MEN and of ANGELS, but have not Love, I have become sounding Brass or a noisy Cymbal.

And if I have ‡Prophecy, and know all SECRETS and All KNOWLEDGE, and if I have All Faith, so as to remove Mountains, but have not Love, I am nothing.

‡If I distribute all my POSSESSIONS in feeding the poor, and if I deliver up my BODY to be burned, but have not Love, I am profited nothing.

‡LOVE suffers long and is kind. LOVE does not envy. LOVE is not boastful; is not puffed up;

acts not unbecomingly, ‡seeks not *THAT which is not HER OWN; is not provoked to anger; does not impute EVIL;

‡rejoices not with INIQUITY, ‡but rejoices with the TRUTH;

covers all things; believes all things; hopes for all things; endures all things.

LOVE fails not at any time; but if there be "Prophecyings," they will be done away; or if, "Languages," they will cease; or if, "Knowledge," it will be made useless.

I Corinthians 8:1–8

Love reckons hours for months, And days for years: And every little absence is an age.

Dryden: Amphitryon

Many waters cannot quench love, neither can the floods drown it: if a man would give all the substance of his house for love, it would utterly be condemned.

Song Of Solomon 8:7

Love conquers all things

Vergil: Eclogues

My bounty is as boundless as the sea,
My love as deep: the more I give to thee
The more I have, for both are infinite.

Shakespeare: Romeo and Juliet

Ye have heard that it hath been said, Thou shalt love thy neighbour, and hate thine enemy.

But I say unto you, Love your enemies, bless them that curse you, do good to them that hate you, and pray for them which despitefully use you, and persecute you;

That ye may be the children of your Father which is in heaven: for he maketh his sun to rise on the evil and on the good, and sendeth rain on the just and on the unjust.

For if ye love them which love you, what reward have ye? do not even the publicans the same?

Matthew 5:43–46

If ye keep my commandments, ye shall abide in my love; even as I have kept my Father's commandments, and abide in his love.

John 15:10

And to know the love of Christ, which passeth knowledge, that ye might be filled with all the fulness of God.

Ephesians 3:19

Honour thy father and thy mother: and, thou shalt love thy neighbour as thyself.

Matthew 19:19

He that loveth not knoweth not God; for God is love.

I John 4:8

Better is a dinner of herbs where love is, than a stalled ox and hatred therewith.

Proverbs 15:17

Finally, brethren, farewell. Be perfect, be of good comfort, be of one mind, live in peace; and the God of love and peace shall be with you.

II Corinthians 13:11

Nevertheless let every one of you in particular so love his wife even as himself; and the wife see that she reverence her husband.

Ephesians 5:33

Let love be without dissimulation. Abhor that which is evil; cleave to that which is good.

Be kindly affectioned one to another with brotherly love; in honour preferring one another;

Romans 12:9, 10

Love worketh no ill to his neighbour: therefore love is the fulfilling of the law.

Romans 13:10

But the fruit of the Spirit is love, joy, peace, longsuffering, gentleness, goodness, faith.

Galatians 5:22

And this I pray, that your love may abound yet more and more in knowledge and in all judgement;

Philippians 1:9

Husbands, love your wives, and be not bitter against them.

Colossians 3:19

In this was manifested the love of God toward us, because that God sent his only begotten Son into the world, that we might live through him.

Herein is love, not that we loved God, but that he loved us, and sent his Son to be the propitiation for our sins.

Beloved, if God so loved us, we ought also to love one another.

I John 4:9–11

There is no fear in love; but perfect love casteth out fear: because fear hath torment. He that feareth is not made perfect in love.

I John 4:18

For the love of money is the root of all evil: which while some coveted after, they have erred from the faith, and pierced themselves through many sorrows.

I Timothy 6:10

My little children, let us not love in word, neither in tongue; but in deed and in truth.

I John 3:18

Howbeit when he, the Spirit of truth, is come, he will guide you into all truth: for he shall not speak of himself; but whatsoever he shall hear, that shall he speak: and he will shew you things to come.

John 16:13

We love him, because he first loved us.

If a man say, I love God, and hateth his brother, he is a liar: for he that loveth not his brother whom he hath seen, how can he love God whom he hath not seen?

And this commandment have we from him, That he who loveth God love his brother also.

I John 4:19–21

For this is the love of God, that we keep his commandments: and his commandments are not grievous.

I John 5:3

And to know the love of Christ, which passeth knowledge, that ye might be filled with all the fulness of God.

Ephesians 3:19

For God so loved the world, that he gave his only begotten Son, that whosoever believeth in him should not perish, but have everlasting life.

John 3:16

He prayeth best who loveth best
All things both great and small:
For the dear God who loveth us,
He made and loveth all.

Coleridge: The Ancient Mariner

Justice

He hath shewed thee, O man, what *is* good; and what doth the Lord require of thee, but to do justly, and to love mercy, and to walk humbly with thy God?

Micah 6:8

And one of the malefactors which were hanged railed on him, saying, If thou be Christ, save thyself and us.

But the other answering rebuked him, saying, Dost not thou fear God, seeing thou art in the same condemnation?

And we indeed justly; for we receive the due reward of our deeds: but this man hath done nothing amiss.

Luke 23:39–41

Touching the Almighty, we cannot find him out:
he is excellent in power, and in judgment, and in
plenty of justice: he will not afflict.

Job 37:23

Defend the poor and fatherless: do justice to the
afflicted and needy.

Psalm 82:3

Justice and judgment are the habitation of thy
throne: mercy and truth shall go before thy face.

Psalm 89:14

If thou seest the oppression of the poor, and violent perverting of judgment and justice in a province, marvel not at the matter: for *he that is* higher than the highest regardeth; and *there be* higher than they.

Ecclesiastes 5:8

For unto us a child is born, unto us a son is given: and the government shall be upon his shoulder: and his name shall be called Wonderful, Counsellor, The mighty God, The everlasting Father, The Prince of Peace.

Of the increase of *his* government and peace *there shall be* no end . . . to order it, and to establish it with judgment and with justice from henceforth even for ever. The zeal of the Lord of hosts will perform this.

Isaiah 9:6–7

Then shalt thou call, and the Lord shall answer; thou shalt cry, and he shall say, Here I *am*. If thou take away from the midst of thee the yoke, the putting forth of the finger, and speaking vanity;

Isaiah 58:9

Thou shalt not wrest judgment; thou shalt not respect persons, neither take a gift: for a gift doth blind the eyes of the wise, and pervert the words of the righteous.

That which is altogether just shalt thou follow, that thou mayest live, and inherit the land which the Lord thy God giveth thee.

Deuteronomy 16:19–20

But thou shalt have a perfect and just weight, a perfect and just measure shalt thou have: that thy days may be lengthened in the land which the Lord thy God giveth thee.

Deuteronomy 25:15

He is the Rock, his work *is* perfect: for all his ways *are* judgment: a God of truth and without iniquity, just and right *is* he.

Deuteronomy 32:4

I can of mine own self do nothing: as I hear, I judge: and my judgment is just; because I seek not mine own will, but the will of the Father which hath sent me.

John 5:30

Let justice be done, though the heavens fall.

Rex vs Wilkes 1768

Only the actions of the just
Smell sweet and blossom in their dust.

James Shirley

Justice without force is powerless; force without justice is tyrannical.

Pascal: Pensées

Wisdom

For in real life, this is the way we've always arrived at decisions, even though it has always been done in a disorganized way. We pass the word around; we ponder how the case is put by different people; we read the poetry; we meditate over the literature; we play music; we change our minds; we reach an understanding. Society evolves this way, not by shouting each other down, but by the unique capacity of unique, individual human beings to comprehend each other.

Dr. Lewis Thomas
From THE MEDUSA
AND THE SNAIL

But where shall wisdom be found? and where *is* the place of understanding?

Man knoweth not the price thereof; neither is it found in the land of the living.

The depth saith, It *is* not in me: and the sea saith, *It is* not with me.

It cannot be gotten for gold, either shall silver be weighed *for* the price thereof.

Whence then cometh wisdom? and where *is* the place of understanding?

And unto man he said, Behold, the fear of the Lord, that *is* wisdom; and to depart from evil is understanding.

Job 28:12–15, 20, 28

In that night did God appear unto Solomon, and said unto him, Ask what I shall give thee.

And Solomon said unto God,

Give me now wisdom and knowledge, that I may go out and come in before this people: for who can judge this thy people, *that is so* great?

And God said to Solomon, Because this was in thine heart, and thou hast not asked riches, wealth, or honour, nor the life of thine enemies, either yet hast asked long life; but hast asked wisdom and knowledge for thyself, that thou mayest judge my people, over whom I have made thee king:

Wisdom and knowledge *is* granted unto thee; and I will give thee riches, and wealth, and honour, such as none of the kings have had that *have been* before thee, neither shall there any after thee have the like.

II Chronicles 1:7–12

I said, Days should speak, and multitude of years should teach wisdom.

But *there is* a spirit in man: and the inspiration of the Almighty giveth them understanding.

Great men are not *always* wise: neither do the aged understand judgment.

Job 32:7–9

And they shall beat their swords into plowshares, and their spears into pruninghooks: nation shall not lift up sword against nation, neither shall they learn war any more.

Isaiah 2:4

Behold, I have taught you statutes and judgments, even as the Lord my God commanded me, that ye should do so in the land whither you go to possess it.

Keep therefore and do *them*; for this *is* your wisdom and your understanding in the sight of the nations, which shall hear all these statutes, and say, Surely this great nation *is* a wise and understanding people.

Deuteronomy 4:5–6

So teach *us* to number our days, that we may apply *our* hearts unto wisdom.

Psalms 90:12

The wolf also shall swell with the lamb, and the leopard shall lie down with the kid; and the calf and the young lion and the fatling together; and a little child shall lead them.

And the cow and the bear shall feed; their young ones shall lie down together: and the lion shall eat straw like the ox.

And the sucking child shall play on the hole of the asp, and the weaned child shall put his hand on the cockatrice' den.

They shall not hurt nor destroy in all my holy mountain: for the earth shall be full of the knowledge of the Lord, as the waters cover the sea.

Isaiah 11:6–9

Get wisdom, get understanding: forget *it* not; neither decline from the words of my mouth.

Forsake her not, and she shall preserve thee: love her, and she shall keep thee.

Wisdom *is* the principal thing; *therefore* get wisdom: and with all thy getting get understanding.

Proverbs 4:5–7

He that getteth wisdom loveth his own soul: he that keepeth understanding shall find good.

Proverbs 19:8

When pride cometh, then cometh shame: but with the lowly *is* wisdom.

Proverbs 11:2

O the depth of the riches both of the wisdom and knowledge of God! how unsearchable *are* his judgments, and his ways past finding out!

For who hath known the mind of the Lord? or who hath been his counsellor?

Romans 11:33–34

Because the foolishness of God is wiser than men; and the weakness of God is stronger than men.

I Corinthians 1:25

Humble yourselves in the sight of the Lord, and he shall lift you up.

James 4:10

Who *is* a wise man and endued with knowledge
among you? let him shew out of a good
conversation his works with meekness of wisdom

But the wisdom that is from above is first pure,
then peaceable, gentle, *and* easy to be intreated,
full of mercy and good fruits, without partiality,
and without hypocrisy.

James 3:13, 17

Go to now, ye that say, To day or to morrow we will go into such a city, and continue there a year, and buy and sell, and get gain:

Whereas ye know not what *shall be* on the morrow. For what *is* your life? It is even a vapour, that appeareth for a little time, and then vanisheth away.

For that ye *ought* to say, If the Lord will, we shall live, and do this, or that.

James 4:13–15

For the goodman *is* not at home, he is gone a long journey:

Proverbs 7:19

If any of you lack wisdom, let him ask of God, that giveth to all *men* liberally, and upbraideth not; and it shall be given him.

James 1:5

That your faith should not stand in the wisdom of men, but in the power of God.

I Corinthians 2:5

For we which live are always delivered unto death for Jesus' sake, that the life also of Jesus might be made manifest in our mortal flesh.

II Corinthians 4:11

But above all things, my brethren, swear not, neither by heaven, neither by the earth, neither by any other oath: but let your yea be yea; and your nay, nay;

James 5:12

Is any among you afflicted? let him pray. Is any merry? let him sing psalms.

Is any sick among you? let him call for the elders of the church; and let them pray over him, anointing him with oil in the name of the Lord:

And the prayer of faith shall save the sick, and the Lord shall raise him up; and if he have committed sins, they shall be forgiven him.

James 5:13–15

Power

Remember that thou magnify his work, which men behold.

Job 36:24

Withhold not good from them to whom it is due, when it is in the power of thine hand to do it.

Say not unto thy neighbour, Go, and come again, and to morrow I will give; when thou hast it by thee.

Proverbs 3:27, 28

God *is* my strength *and* power: and he maketh my way perfect.

II Samuel 22:33

Hast thou not known? hast thou not heard, *that* the everlasting God, the Lord, the Creator of the ends of the earth, fainteth not, neither is weary? *there is* no searching of his understanding.

He giveth power to the faint; and to *them that have* no might he increaseth strength.

Even the youths shall fain and be weary, and the young men shall utterly fall:

But they that wait upon the Lord shall renew *their* strength; they shall mount up with wings as eagles; they shall run, and not be weary; *and* they shall walk, and not faint.

Isaiah 40:28–31

I have seen the wicked in great power, and spreading himself like a green bay tree.

Yet he passed away, and, lo, he *was not*: yea, I sought him, but he could not be found.

Mark the perfect *man*, and behold the upright: for the end of *that* man is peace.

Psalm 37:35–37

Now also when I am old and greyheaded, O God, forsake me not; until I have shewed thy strength unto *this* generation, *and* thy power to every one *that* is to come.

Psalm 71:18

Thine, O Lord, is the greatness, and the power, and the glory, and the victory, and the majesty: for all *that is* in the heaven and in the earth is *thine*; thine *is* the kingdom, O Lord, and thou art exalted as head above all.

Both riches and honour *come* of thee, and thou reignest over all; and in thine hand *is* power and might; and in thine hand *it is* to make great, and to give strength unto all.

I Chronicles 29:11, 12

He divideth the sea with his power, and by his understanding he smiteth through the proud.

Job 26:12

Shall I not, as I have done unto Sa-ma-ri-a and her idols, so do to Jerusalem and her idols?

Isaiah 10:11

And the work of the righteous shall be peace; and the effect of righteousness quietness and assurance for ever.

Isaiah 32:17

But I *am* the Lord thy God, that divided the sea, whose waves roared: The Lord of hosts *is* his name.

Isaiah 51:15

For God, who commanded the light to shine out of darkness, hath shined in our hearts, to *give* the light of the knowledge of the glory of God in the face of Jesus Christ.

But we have this treasure in earthen vessels, that the excellency of the power may be of God, and not of us.

We are troubled on every side, yet not distressed; *we are* perplexed, but not in despair;

Persecuted, but not forsaken; cast down, but not destroyed;

II Corinthians 4:6–9

Desiring to be teachers of the law; understanding neither what they say, nor whereof they affirm.

I Timothy 1:7

All things are lawful unto me, but all things are not expedient: all things are lawful for me, but I will not be brought under the power of any.

I Corinthians 6:12

People are always blaming their circumstances for what they are. I don't believe in circumstances. The people who get on in this world are the people who get up and look for the circumstances they want, and, if they can't find them, make them.

George Bernard Shaw
MRS. WARREN'S
PROFESSION
Act II, 1893

When society requires to be rebuilt, there is no use in attempting to rebuild it on the old plan. No great improvements in the lot of mankind are possible, until a great change takes place in the fundamental constitution of their modes of thought.

John Stuart Mill

Every man takes the limits of his own field of vision for the limits of the world.

Arthur Schopenhauer

For unto whomsoever much is given, of him shall be much required: And to whom men have committed much, of him they will ask the more.

Luke, 12:48

Rilke *never* said I give you the answers. He said love the questions and perhaps you'll live your way into the answers.

Rainer Maria Rilke
Introduction from
DUINO ELEGIES
Translated by Gary Miranda

This, therefore, is a faded dream of the time when I went down into the dust and noise of the eastern market-place, and with my brain and muscles, with sweat and constant thinking, made others see my visions coming true. Those who dream by night in the dusty recesses of their minds wake in the day to find that all was vanity; but the dreamers of the day are dangerous men, for they may act their dream with open eyes, and make it possible.

T. E. Lawrence
Introduction to
SEVEN PILLARS OF
WISDOM

If I were to wish for anything, I should not wish for wealth and power, but for the passionate sense of the potential, for the eye which, ever young and ardent, sees the possible. Pleasure disappoints, possibility never. And what wine is so sparkling, what so fragrant, what so intoxicating as possibility!

Kierkegaard
EITHER/OR

Life cannot wait until the sciences have explained the universe. We cannot put off living until we are ready. The most salient characteristic of life is its coerciveness; it is always urgent, "here and now" without any possible postponement. Life is fired at us point blank.

Jose Ortega Y. Gasset

Courage is the price life exacts for granting peace. The soul that knows it not Knows no release from Little things.

Amelia Earhart